# DEADLY AND INCREDIBLE ANIMALS

## TOP 10 Birds of Prey

**Jay Dale**

A+

Smart Apple Media
P.O. Box 3263
Mankato, MN, 56002

First published in 2011 by
MACMILLAN EDUCATION AUSTRALIA PTY LTD
15–19 Claremont St, South Yarra, Australia 3141

Visit our web site at www.macmillan.com.au or go directly to
www.macmillanlibrary.com.au

Associated companies and representatives throughout the world.

Copyright text © Jay Dale 2011

Dale, Jay.
Top ten birds of prey / Jay Dale.
    p. cm. — (Deadly and incredible animals)
  Includes index.
  Summary: "Gives general information on features of birds of prey and threats to them. Counts down the top ten most dangerous birds of prey using a deadliness scale"—Provided by publisher.
  ISBN 978-1-59920-408-6 (library binding)
  1. Birds of prey—Juvenile literature. I. Title.
  QL677.78.D35 2012
598.9—dc22

                    2010049501

Publisher: Carmel Heron
Commissioning Editor: Niki Horin
Managing Editor: Vanessa Lanaway
Proofreader: Georgina Garner
Designer: Cristina Neri, Canary Graphic Design
Page layout: Peter Shaw, Julie Thompson and Cristina Neri
Photo researcher: Legendimages
Illustrators: Andrew Craig and Nives Porcellato
Production Controller: Vanessa Johnson

Manufactured in China by Macmillan Production (Asia) Ltd.
Kwun Tong, Kowloon, Hong Kong
Supplier Code: CP February 2011

**Acknowledgments**
The author and publisher are grateful to the following for permission to reproduce copyright material:

Front cover photograph: Lappetfaced Vulture, South Africa © iStockphoto/Johan Swanepoel.

Photographs courtesy of: ardea.com/Kenneth W. Fink, **27**; Corbis/John Carnemolla, **16**, /Anup Shah, **11**; Dreamstime.com/Drevil5000, **25**, /Outdoorsman, **6** (top), /Zandebasenjis, **24**; Getty Images/Jim Brandenburg, **23**, /Klaus Nigge, **18**; iStockphoto/alarifoto, **4**, /Stuart Berman, **20**, /Johan Swanepoel, **10**; NASA, **14**, /Gary Rothstein, **5**; National Geographic Stock/Klaus Nigge, **19**; Photolibrary/ Alamy/Emil Enchev, **21**, /Alamy/Papilio, **28**, /Alaska Stock Images, **13**, /Piers Cavendish, **30**, /John Downer, **29**, /Ken M Johns, **8**, /Mark Jones, **26**, /Alessandra Sarti, **17**, /Gunter Ziesler, **9**; Shutterstock/Walter G Arce, **6** (center), /David Davis, **22**, /DD Photography, **15** (background), /FloridaStock, **12**, /Lone Wolf Photos, **7**, /pix2go, **3**, **15**, /S.Cooper Digital, **6** (center).

While every care has been taken to trace and acknowledge copyright, the publisher tenders their apologies for any accidental infringement where copyright has proved untraceable. They would be pleased to come to a suitable arrangement with the rightful owner in each case.

The author would like to thank Sharnika Blacker for helping with the research on this book.

# CONTENTS

**GLOSSARY WORDS**
When a word is printed in **bold**, you can look up its meaning in the Glossary on page 31.

# DEADLY AND INCREDIBLE ANIMALS

Many animals are deadly to other animals. They are deadly to their prey and sometimes even to their **predators**. Over many thousands of years, these animals have developed incredible behaviors and features to find food, to defend themselves from predators, and to protect their young.

## Deadly and Incredible Features and Behaviors

Different types of animals have different deadly features and behaviors. Deadly and incredible features include strong jaws, razor-sharp teeth, and stingers or fangs for injecting **venom** into prey. Deadly and incredible behaviors include stalking, hunting, and distracting prey before attacking and killing it.

Animals such as lions use their incredible size and strength to smash, crush, and rip apart their prey. Excellent eyesight helps many **nocturnal** animals hunt their prey under the cover of even the darkest night.

◄ Birds of prey, such as this golden eagle, use their sharp beaks to rip their prey apart.

# DEADLY AND INCREDIBLE BIRDS OF PREY

Some of the world's most deadly and incredible birds glide high in the sky or swoop silently in the night.

## What Are Birds of Prey?

Birds of prey, also known as raptors, are meat-eating birds. This group of birds includes kites, vultures, hawks, eagles, and falcons. Birds of prey are deadly hunters with strong feet, powerful and sharp **talons**, and hooked beaks.

## IN THIS BOOK

In this book you will read about the top 10 deadliest birds of prey on Earth — from number 10 (least deadly) to number 1 (most deadly). There are many different opinions on which birds of prey should top this list. The birds in this book have been selected based on their hunting methods, power, strength, and speed.

The osprey is a skilled flyer and fish-catcher.

## Living Dinosaurs

Many scientists say birds of prey are "living dinosaurs" because they are closely related to meat-eating dinosaurs such as the troodon. Some **dinosaur fossils** with feathers have even been found.

# FEATURES OF BIRDS OF PREY

Birds of prey have many deadly and incredible features and behaviors in common. These features help birds of prey to survive in the environments in which they live.

## Talons

A bird of prey's **talons** are incredibly sharp and are used to grab, **stun**, and kill its prey. They are also used for perching and balancing on trees.

▶ The golden eagle's talons are used for tearing prey into smaller pieces.

## Beak

The beak of a bird of prey is typically large, with the upper beak curving over the end of the lower beak, like a hook.

◀ The bald eagle's beak is sharp and strong, and can rip its prey apart.

## Eyesight

Most birds of prey have incredible **binocular vision**, enabling them to see things far away.

▶ The great horned owl has incredible eyesight and can see its prey many hundreds of feet away.

## Wings

Birds of prey have a large **wingspan,** which helps them glide. They are very accurate, fast, and skilled flyers.

## WINGSPAN OF THE TOP TEN DEADLIEST BIRDS OF PREY

| Bird of Prey | Wingspan |
| --- | --- |
| Peregrine falcon | 2.5 to 4 feet (0.8–1.2 m) |
| Great horned owl | 4 feet (1.2 m) |
| Crowned hawk-eagle | 5 to 7 feet (1.5–2.1 m) |
| Golden eagle | 5 to 8 feet (1.5–2.4 m) |
| Wedge-tailed eagle | 6 to 7 feet (1.8–2.2 m) |
| Harpy eagle | 6.5 feet (2 m) |
| Osprey | 6.5 feet (2 m) |
| Philippine eagle | 6.5 feet (2 m) |
| Bald eagle | 8 feet (2.4 m) |
| Lappet-faced vulture | 10 feet (3 m) |

◄ Birds of prey can fly silently, without flapping their wings. This is called gliding.

# THREATS TO BIRDS OF PREY

Many birds of prey are high in the **food chain** and have no animal predators. Their only real threats are human activities.

## Hunting

The shooting or hunting of birds of prey is now illegal in many countries, but this sport was responsible for killing many birds. Shooting birds of prey still occurs, especially around farms where farmers want to protect their animals from the birds.

## Farming Chemicals

A poison used on farm crops called DDT (dichloro-diphenyl-trichloroethane) is a threat to birds of prey. If the prey the bird feeds on has eaten some of this poison, it can be very harmful to the bird. Over time, DDT has caused some birds' eggshells to become so soft that they break when parents sit on them in the nest.

Birds of prey that nest around farmland may be affected by chemicals, such as DDT, or shot by farmers.

## Threats to Survival

Many birds of prey **species** have become **extinct** and others are **endangered**. The Guadalupe caracaras, a falcon, became extinct in the early 1900s due to hunting by farmers who were protecting their goat herds.

The Cuban kite, Madagascar fish-eagle and Philippine eagle are just three of many birds of prey that are critically endangered (at extremely high risk of becoming extinct). More than 150 species of birds of prey have been recognized as being under threat: vulnerable, near threatened, endangered, critically endangered, or extinct.

## SOME BIRDS OF PREY UNDER THREAT

| Bird of Prey | Threat Level | Bird of Prey | Threat Level |
|---|---|---|---|
| Bald eagle | | Osprey | |
| Wedge-tailed eagle | Least concern — no threat to their survival | Golden eagle | Least concern — no threat to their survival |
| Great horned owl | | Peregrine falcon | |
| Crowned hawk-eagle | | Lappet-faced vulture | Vulnerable — likely to become endangered unless it is more protected |
| Harpy eagle | Near threatened — may need protection in the future | Philippine eagle | Critically endangered — at high risk of becoming extinct |

▶ The Philippine eagle is threatened in the wild because of the destruction of its natural forest **habitat** and hunting.

# LAPPET-FACED VULTURE

With a wingspan of 10 feet (3 m) and a large, hooked beak, the lappet-faced vulture is a frightening sight. Even cheetahs stay away from this deadly and **aggressive** bird.

broad wings

bald head, with loose flaps of skin (lappets)

good eyesight

large, hooked beak

## That's Incredible!

The lappet-faced vulture can strip a dead antelope to the bone in about 20 minutes.

talons

▲ The lappet-faced vulture gets its name from the overlapping and hanging flaps of skin (lappets) on its bare, pink head.

**Deadly features:** large size, good eyesight, weight, wingspan, sharp beak, and aggressive nature

**Predators:** crows, eagles

**Size:** weight up to 31 pounds (14 kg); length 45 inches (115 cm); wingspan 10 feet (3 m)

**Lifespan:** 40 years

**Habitat:** desert, grasslands

**Distribution:** ■
Middle East, desert and grassland regions in northern Africa, as well as eastern and southern Africa

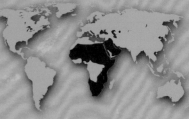

## Scavenger and Opportunistic Hunter

Vultures are often thought of as scavengers — animals that eat the leftover remains of other predators' kill. The lappet-faced vulture is a scavenger, but it will also hunt whatever is around it. This is called opportunistic hunting. It will attack and kill young gazelles, antelopes, and flamingos. It will also steal young birds and eggs from nests, and eat termites as they come out of their mounds.

## An Aggressive Chaser

The lappet-faced vulture is aggressive — it will run toward other predators and their kill with its head lowered, neck outstretched and wings spread. It chases other scavengers, such as jackals and smaller vultures, away from its prey and eats as much as it wants.

### What's for Dinner?

Lappet-faced vultures eat **carrion**, eggs, termites, locusts, young birds, gazelles, antelopes, and flamingos.

◀ The lappet-faced vulture has excellent eyesight and can locate leftover animal remains 1 mile (1.6 km) away.

# BALD EAGLE

The bald eagle can see seven times better than most humans. It uses its excellent eyesight, including **peripheral vision** and binocular vision, to see small movements great distances away.

light but strong wings

excellent eyesight

hooked beak

mighty wings

large, powerful talons

strong legs

spiny pads

▲ The bald eagle's strong wings and legs allow it to carry large prey.

## That's Incredible!

When a bald eagle loses a feather on one wing, it will balance itself by dropping a feather from the other wing.

**Deadly features:** long and strong talons, powerful legs and wings, excellent eyesight, great speed in flying and diving

**Predators:** ospreys (see page 14)

**Size:** weight 9 to 13 pounds (4–7 kg); length 28 to 43 inches (70–110 cm); wingspan up to 8 feet (2.4 m)

**Lifespan:** 25 to 40 years

**Habitat:** coastlines, lakes, rivers, swamps, and marshes

**Distribution:** ■
Canada, United States, northwest Mexico

## High Flyer

The bald eagle has light, strong wings that are built for power and speed. It can **soar** to great heights. It can also fly incredible distances without flapping its wings. When diving for prey, it can reach speeds of up to 200 miles (322 km) per hour.

## Watch, Wait, Attack!

The bald eagle is an aggressive hunter. It can spend hours perched in a tree overlooking water, waiting for a fish to move near the surface. At the smallest sign of movement, it swoops down with amazing speed to snatch the fish in its talons.

### What's for Dinner?

Bald eagles usually eat fish, but sometimes eat other birds, rabbits, snakes, rodents, and young deer.

▲ The bald eagle carries its prey back to its perch and eats it with its strong, sharp beak.

# OSPREY

The osprey (also known as the sea hawk or fish eagle) is a precise and deadly hunter. It dives feet-first into water and catches fish in its talons.

long, narrow wings

▶ The osprey uses its long, narrow wings to fly in circles high above the water, on the lookout for prey.

sharp, hooked beak

backward-facing scales to help grip prey

curved, hooked talons

## That's Incredible!

The osprey sometimes flies low and very slowly over calm waters, dangling its feet in and out of the water. This makes fish move or jump, so the osprey knows exactly where to target its prey.

**Deadly features:** curved talons and spiky foot scales, speed, underwater ability, strength, excellent eyesight

**Predators:** foxes, skunks, raccoons, crows, vultures, and bald eagles

**Size:** weight 4 pounds (2 kg); length 24 inches (60 cm); wingspan up to 6.5 feet (2 m)

**Lifespan:** 20 to 25 years

**Habitat:** varied, but usually close to salt or fresh water

**Distribution:** ■ worldwide — northern birds will migrate south over winter

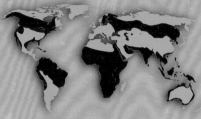

## High Diver

The osprey seeks out its meal while flying. It **hovers** over water, then suddenly dives feet-first right into the water, reappearing with a fish held firmly in its talons. It can dive from heights of 33 to 131 feet (10–40 m).

**What's for Dinner?**

Ospreys eat mostly fish (99 percent of the time), as well as some small mammals, snakes, and reptiles.

## Fishhook Talons

The osprey has curved talons, which look like fishhooks. When an osprey catches a fish, it uses both feet—one in front of the other. It places two claws on either side of the fish. It carries the fish headfirst and flies away quickly.

◀ The osprey's sharp, hooked beak is ideal for ripping and pulling apart its prey.

# WEDGE-TAILED EAGLE

The wedge-tailed eagle (or eaglehawk) is one of the largest birds of prey. This graceful but deadly raptor swoops down from the skies, grabbing its prey in its large talons. It is strong enough to carry prey half its own weight.

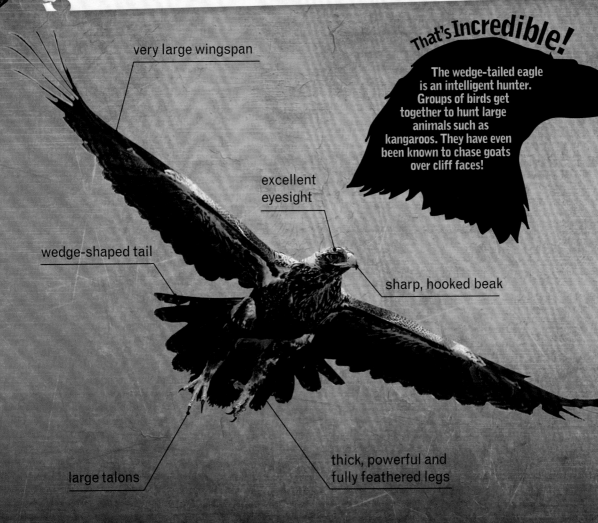

very large wingspan

## That's Incredible!

The wedge-tailed eagle is an intelligent hunter. Groups of birds get together to hunt large animals such as kangaroos. They have even been known to chase goats over cliff faces!

excellent eyesight

wedge-shaped tail

sharp, hooked beak

large talons

thick, powerful and fully feathered legs

▲ The wedge-tailed eagle is easily identified by its wedge-shaped tail and long, broad wings.

**Deadly features:** large talons, hooked beak, excellent eyesight, large wingspan for gliding and stalking prey, thick and powerful legs

**Predators:** humans

**Size:** weight 7 to 13 pounds (3–6 kg); length 31 to 41 inches (80–104 cm); wingspan 6 to 7 feet (1.8–2.2 m)

**Lifespan:** up to 20 years

**Habitat:** open forest, open plains, and mountains

**Distribution:** ■
Australia and southern New Guinea

## Eagle-eyed Hunter

The wedge-tailed eagle has incredible eyesight, enabling it to carefully work out distances. Its eyes are surrounded by bony rings, which squeeze to make its eyeballs longer. This enlarges what the bird actually sees. It has the unique ability to "see" warm and cold air currents, which it uses to easily fly high or drift downward.

### What's for Dinner?

Wedge-tailed eagles eat ground-dwelling animals, such as rabbits, young sheep, and kangaroos. They also scavenge leftover remains by roadsides.

## Gliding Attack

The wedge-tailed eagle usually catches its prey on the ground in a gliding attack. It travels great distances in search of prey, soaring with its massive wings outstretched. Once it sees the prey, it sweeps down gracefully to snatch up its victim in its sharp talons.

▶ The wedge-tailed eagle uses its strong, sharp claws and sharp beak to rip its prey to pieces.

# PHILIPPINE EAGLE

The Philippine eagle (also known as the great Philippine eagle or monkey-eating eagle) has long, sharp talons that enable it to pull out prey from inside tree hollows.

## That's Incredible!

Young Philippine eagles have been known to attack non-living objects when practising their hunting techniques. They also try to hang upside down in order to work on their balance!

▶ The Philippine eagle is one of the tallest, largest and most powerful raptors in the world.

shaggy **crest**

curved beak

short, broad wings

long talons

powerful legs

**Deadly features:** large size and weight, long talons, sharp curved beak

**Predators:** none

**Size:** weight 15 pounds (7 kg); length 3 feet (1 m); wingspan 6.5 feet (2 m)

**Lifespan:** 30 to 60 years

**Habitat:** tropical low-lying and mountainous forests

**Distribution:** ■
Philippines (on eastern Luzon, Samar, Leyte and Mindanao islands)

## Agile Hunter

The Philippine eagle is well suited to hunting in forests. It weaves through the trees in search of prey on the ground and up in the trees. Its wingspan is not as big as the wingspan of raptors that hunt in open areas. However, its wings are broader and rounder, making it easier to fly and dart through forested areas.

## Monkey Business

Philippine eagles sometimes work in pairs to hunt troops of monkeys. One eagle will perch on a branch to distract the monkeys while the other swoops in for the kill, often going unnoticed.

### What's for Dinner?

Philippine eagles eat birds, flying lemurs, monkeys, deer, pigs, dogs (occasionally), large bats, and snakes.

▼ Although Philippine eagles sometimes work together to catch prey, they will also fight over the meat, as these two birds are doing.

# GOLDEN EAGLE

The talons of a golden eagle are believed to be stronger than a human's hand and arm. There are reports that golden eagles have hunted and carried away bear cubs.

large, broad wings

large eyes with excellent eyesight

**That's Incredible!**

In Kazakhstan, in central Asia, nomadic hunters tame and train golden eagles to hunt wolves, deer, and antelope.

beak

powerful, sharp talons

▲ The golden eagle is not really golden, but has dark brown plumage and bright yellow talons.

**Deadly features:** powerful talons, excellent eyesight, speed of flight, size, weight, power

**Predators:** lions, leopards, hyenas, and wild dogs

**Size:** weight 6 to 15 pounds (2.5–7 kg); length 24 to 39 inches (65–100 cm); wingspan 5 to 8 feet (1.5–2.4 m)

**Lifespan:** up to 38 years in the wild (50 years in zoos)

**Habitat:** mountainous areas

**Distribution:** ■ Europe, central and northern Asia, northern Africa, North America, and Japan

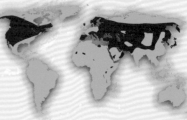

## Deadly Accurate

The golden eagle is a swift and accurate hunter. When diving through the air to attack prey, it can reach speeds of 120 miles (193 km) per hour. Even large prey is killed instantly when it is struck by the golden eagle's powerful feet and talons. The eagle usually attacks its prey on the ground, but it has been known to attack geese and diving ducks in mid-air.

### What's for Dinner?

Golden eagles eat other birds, foxes, young deer, caribou (large deer), and bear cubs.

◄ The golden eagle's beak is used solely for tearing up and eating its prey.

## Hunting in Pairs

A pair of golden eagles (male and female) will stay together for life. They defend their nest together. Golden eagle pairs have been observed in exciting acrobatic displays protecting their nests from other birds. Often they will hunt together, with one driving the prey toward its partner, who will then attack and kill the prey.

# GREAT HORNED OWL

The great horned owl is one of the fiercest birds in the sky. This terrifying bird of prey has even been known to frighten a bald eagle away from its nest.

horn-like tufts of feathers

large eyes

hooked beak

camouflaged plumage

large talons

## That's Incredible!

The great horned owl often eats its prey whole. Strong stomach juices break down the prey. Bones, fur, and teeth are turned into pellets, which the owl brings up 8 to 12 hours later.

◀ The great horned owl's large, powerful talons are used to kill, carry, and rip apart its prey.

softly fringed wings

**Deadly features:** excellent night vision, excellent hearing, silent flight, camouflaged plumage, large talons

**Predators:** foxes, coyotes, and feral cats

**Size:** weight 3 pounds (1.4 kg); length 22 inches (55 cm); wingspan 4 feet (1.2 m)

**Lifespan:** 15 to 20 years

**Habitat:** varied — forests, deserts, open country, swamps, and even city parks

**Distribution:** ■
Arctic, North America, Central America, and South America

## Night Vision

The great horned owl's large, forward-looking eyes give it binocular vision. This owl can see 50 to 100 times better than humans in dull light. The great horned owl also has amazing hearing. It can hunt by sound, which is useful when the night is pitch black.

## Surprise Attack

The great horned owl usually hunts at sunrise and sunset. Its gray–brown feathers camouflage it against the bark of trees. The owl's soft-edged feathers allow it to fly in silence, without flapping. When the owl locates its prey, it glides down to snatch it up in its powerful talons, often killing the prey instantly.

### What's for Dinner?
Great horned owls eat small to medium animals, including birds, fish, and even skunks and scorpions!

▶ The great horned owl's incredible eyesight and excellent hearing make it a deadly nocturnal predator.

23

# PEREGRINE FALCON

The peregrine falcon is one of the most common birds of prey in the world. It can dive at speeds of more than 200 miles (320 km) per hour, making it the fastest creature on Earth.

notched upper beak

extra eyelid, for keeping eyeball moist

**That's Incredible!**

The peregrine falcon plucks the feathers out of its prey with its powerful talons and sharp beak before ripping the prey apart.

hooked talons

long, tapered wings

▲ The peregrine falcon can use its strong upper beak to break the neck of its prey.

**Deadly features:** speed, powerful hooked talons, notched beak

**Predators:** raccoons, great horned owls, humans

**Size:** weight 1 to 3 pounds (0.5 –1.5 kg); length 14 to 24 inches (34–58 cm); wingspan 2.5 to 4 feet (0.8 –1.2 m)

**Lifespan:** up to 15.5 years

**Habitat:** varied — mountain ranges, semi-desert regions, coastal cliffs, city buildings

**Distribution:** ■
all continents
except
Antarctica

## Flying Attack

The peregrine falcon attacks birds mid-flight. It folds back its tail and wings and tucks its feet under itself before swooping down on birds from above. It clenches its foot like a fist, then strikes its prey, which stuns or kills it. The falcon turns and catches the prey while still in mid-flight.

## Diving Tools

Special features help the peregrine falcon to breathe and see while diving quickly through the air after prey. Small, bony lumps inside its nostrils make it easier to breathe air while diving at high speeds. To protect its eyes, it spreads tears over its eyeballs using its third eyelid.

▼ The peregrine falcon hunts most often at dawn and dusk, when its prey is most active.

### What's for Dinner?
Peregrine falcons mostly eat small and medium-sized birds, and sometimes rabbits, lizards, mice, and rats.

# HARPY EAGLE

The harpy eagle may not be the largest bird of prey in the world, but it is certainly the heaviest and most powerful. Its deadly talons can crush the bones of its prey and kill it instantly.

distinctive feathery crest

► The harpy eagle is a very strong bird. It can use its powerful talons to snatch large prey and fly away with it.

curved beak

thick legs

## That's Incredible!

The harpy eagle's eyesight is so incredible that it can see something that is 1 inch (2 cm) in size from a distance of 650 feet (200 m)!

long, curved talons

**Deadly features:** curved talons up to 5 inches (13 cm) long, powerful grasp, strong legs, weight, size, strength, quick movement, excellent eyesight

**Predators:** jaguars, anacondas, other snakes

**Size:** weight 20 pounds (9 kg); length 41 inches (105 cm); wingspan 6.5 feet (2 m)

**Lifespan:** 25 to 35 years

**Habitat:** tropical forests

**Distribution:** ■
Central and South America, from southern Mexico to northern Argentina

## Patient Hunter

A harpy eagle can spend up to 23 hours perched in a tree waiting for prey to appear. It then swoops down, with outstretched feet, to snatch up the prey with its powerful talons. Its short, broad wings also enable it to fly straight up, to attack its prey from below.

## Bone-breaking Talons

The harpy eagle's talons are up to 5 inches (13 cm) longer than a bear's claws. They have such a powerful grasp that they could break a human's arm.

▼ If its prey is heavy, the harpy eagle will eat part of it on a perch before taking it to its nest.

### What's for Dinner?

Harpy eagles eat monkeys, sloths, deer, large birds, porcupines, iguanas, and snakes.

# CROWNED HAWK-EAGLE

The crowned hawk-eagle's powerful talons are strong enough to crush a monkey's skull, killing it instantly.

## That's Incredible!

The female crowned hawk-eagle lays one or two white, speckled eggs. If two chicks hatch, the stronger one (usually the first to hatch) kills the weaker chick.

large crest

sharp, hooked beak

broad wings

thick legs

▶ The crowned hawk-eagle can be identified by its impressive crest of feathers on top of its head.

hind talons

**Deadly features:** sharp talons (especially on the back toe), powerful legs, weight, size, quick movement

**Predators:** none

**Size:** weight 5.5 to 9 pounds (2.5–4.2 kg); length 31 to 35 inches (80–90 cm); wingspan 5 to 7 feet (1.5–2.1 m)

**Lifespan:** unknown

**Habitat:** forest, rainforest, grassland

**Distribution:** ◼
Tropical Africa south of the Sahara, including Senegal, Kenya, Ethiopia, Angola, Botswana, and South Africa

## Vicious Predator

The crowned hawk-eagle is a vicious predator. It uses its long hind talons to break the spine of its prey. Sometimes it presses down on its victim's throat to stop it breathing. The crowned hawk-eagle has been known to hunt prey weighing up to 77 pounds (35 kg). That's about the average weight of an 11-year-old boy!

## Hunting Pairs

Crowned hawk-eagles often hunt in pairs. The male flies high in the sky and calls out to get the attention of the prey below. The female then flies just above the trees and snatches the distracted prey.

### What's for Dinner?

Crowned hawk-eagles eat monkeys, antelopes, and sometimes smaller animals such as birds, lizards, and snakes – if they cannot find larger animals.

# FALCONRY

**Falconry is a sport where birds of prey are kept and trained to hunt.**

## A Traditional Sport

Falconry was very popular in the Middle Ages (1100–1453 A.D.). Noblemen mostly used falcons, buzzards, and hawks. These birds are trained to hunt animals such as foxes, rabbits, hares, pheasants, and wild turkeys, and bring them back to their masters. In the early stages of training, the birds wear leather hoods, to keep them calm while they get used to being around humans.

## Falconry Today

In some countries, people need a special license to be a falconer and they have to follow very strict rules. To get a license, the person must pass a written test on the rules and also have their equipment and facilities inspected. They might need to spend two years as an apprentice to another licensed falconer.

▶ A falconer wears a thick leather glove, called a gauntlet, to protect his arm from the bird's sharp talons.

# GLOSSARY

**Aggressive** Angry and often ready to attack

**Binocular vision** Using two eyes together

**Camouflaged** Having spots, stripes, other patterns or colors on an animal allowing it to blend in with its environment

**Carrion** Decaying flesh of dead animals

**Crest** Group of feathers on the head

**Dinosaur fossils** Old remains of dinosaurs that are buried under many layers of earth and rock

**Endangered** In danger of becoming extinct

**Extinct** Wiped out, or no longer alive anywhere on Earth

**Food chain** A linked system of animals, plants, and other living things in which each member is eaten in turn by another member

**Habitat** The environment where animals and plants live

**Hind** At the back

**Hovers** Stays still in mid-air

**Nocturnal** Active (usually hunting) at night

**Peripheral vision** Ability to see things to the side, as well as to the front

**Plumage** All the feathers of a bird

**Predators** Meat-eating animals that hunt, kill, and eat other animals

**Soar** To fly upward

**Species** A group of animals or other living things that share similar features and behaviors

**Stun** To knock unconscious or into a daze

**Talons** Thick, strong claws

**Venom** A poisonous or harmful substance produced by an animal, which is injected by a bite or a sting

**Wingspan** Length of wings from the tip of one to the tip of the other

# INDEX